PowerKids Readers:

Bilingual Edition
My Library of Holidays™
Edición Bilingüe

Thanksgiving
Día de Acción de Gracias

May Harte
Traducción al español:
Tomás González

The Rosen Publishing Group's
PowerKids Press™ & **Editorial Buenas Letras**™
New York

1

Published in 2004 by The Rosen Publishing Group, Inc.
29 East 21st Street, New York, NY 10010

First Edition
Book Design: Michael J. Caroleo

Photo Credits: Cover and pp. 11, 22 (harvest) © Jose Luis Pelaez, Inc./CORBIS; p. 5 © Lake County Museum/CORBIS; pp. 7, 9, 13, 22 (Native Americans and Pilgrims) © Bettmann/CORBIS; p. 15 © Ariel Skelley/CORBIS; p 17. © Rick Barrentine/CORBIS; p. 19 © Royalty-Free/CORBIS; pp. 21, 22 (parade) © Kelly-Mooney Photography/CORBIS; p. 22 (cranberry sauce) © Rick Barrentine/CORBIS.

Harte, May
Thanksgiving = Día de acción de gracias / May Harte ; translated by Tomás González.
p. cm. – (My library of holidays)
Includes bibliographical references and index.
Summary: This book explains the American history that led to the observance of our Thanksgiving and describes how our holiday is celebrated.
ISBN 1-4042-7527-4 (lib.)
1. Thanksgiving [1. Thanksgiving 2. Holidays 3. Spanish language materials—Bilingual]
I. Title II. Title: Día de Acción de Gracias III. Series
2004   2003-009822
394.2649—dc21

Manufactured in the United States of America

2

Contents

Contenido

Thanksgiving is an American holiday. Do you know when Thanksgiving began?

El Día de Acción de Gracias es una fiesta norteamericana. ¿Sabes cuándo comenzó?

4

Thanksgiving Day

GREETINGS.

Design Copyright 1910 by Frances Brundage.

James Brundage

5

In 1620, a group of people called the Pilgrims came to America from Europe. They came to find a better life in America.

En 1620, un grupo de personas llamadas peregrinos, llegó a América desde Europa. Los peregrinos vinieron en busca de una vida mejor.

The Pilgrims came on a boat called the *Mayflower*.

Los peregrinos llegaron en un barco llamado *Mayflower*.

9

The Pilgrims found it hard to grow food during their first year in America. In the second year they were able to grow a harvest of good food.

Durante el primer año en América a los peregrinos les resultó difícil cultivar sus alimentos. En el segundo año pudieron obtener una buena cosecha.

In 1621, the Pilgrims had the first Thanksgiving. They gave thanks with the Native Americans who had helped them to grow the food.

En 1621, los peregrinos celebraron el primer Día de Acción de Gracias. Dieron gracias junto con los nativos americanos, quienes les habían ayudado a cultivar sus alimentos.

Today, American families have Thanksgiving on the fourth Thursday of November every year.

Hoy, las familias estadounidenses celebran el Día de Acción de Gracias el cuarto jueves de noviembre de cada año.

People eat a lot of good food at Thanksgiving. Many families eat turkey and cranberry sauce.

La gente disfruta de mucha comida deliciosa el Día de Acción de Gracias. Muchas familias comen pavo con salsa de arándano.

People eat pumpkin pie, too.

También se come pastel de calabaza.

19

Many people go to
Thanksgiving Day parades.
What do you do on
Thanksgiving?

Mucha gente asiste a los
desfiles del Día de Acción
de Gracias. ¿Qué haces tú
ese día?

Words to Know
Palabras que debes saber

cranberry sauce
salsa de arándano

harvest
cosecha

Native Americans
nativos americanos

parade
desfile

Pilgrims
peregrinos

Here are more books to read about Thanksgiving/
Otros libros que puedes leer sobre el Día de
Acción de Gracias:

In English/En inglés:

Countdown to Thanksgiving
by Jodi Huelin, Keiko Motoyama (Illustrator)
Penguin Putnam Books for Young Readers

If You Were at the First Thanksgiving
by Anne Kamma, Bert Dodson (Illustrator)
Scholastic, Inc.

The Thanksgiving Story
by Alice Dalgliesh, Helen Sewell (Illustrator)
Simon & Schuster Children's

Bilingual Books/Libros bilingües:

La historia del Día de Acción de Gracias / The Thanksgiving Story
by Nancy J. Skarmeas, Stacy Venturi-Pickett, Patricia A. Pingryl (Illustrator)
Ideals Publications, Inc.

Due to the changing nature of Internet links,
PowerKids Press has developed an online list
of Web sites related to the subject of this book.
This site is updated regularly. Please use this
link to access the list:

http://www.buenasletraslinks.com/mlholi/dag

Index

Índice

Words in English: 141   Palabras en español: 163

Note to Parents, Teachers, and Librarians

PowerKids Readers books *en español* are specially designed for emergent Hispanic readers and students learning Spanish in the United States. Simple stories and concepts are paired with photographs of real kids in real-life situations. Sentences are short and simple, employing a basic vocabulary of sight words, as well as new words that describe familiar things and places. With their engaging stories and vivid photo-illustrations, PowerKids *en español* gives children the opportunity to develop a love of reading and learning that they will carry with them throughout their lives.

Allison